The I ♥

TRADER JOE'S®
COCKTAIL BOOK

52 Drink Recipes for
Every Occasion Using Ingredients
from the World's Greatest Grocery Store

GREG McBOAT

ULYSSES PRESS

T0274431

Published by:
Ulysses Press
PO Box 3440
Berkeley, CA 94703
www.ulyssespress.com

ISBN: 978-1-64604-702-4
Library of Congress Control Number: 2024934566

Printed in China
10 9 8 7 6 5 4 3 2

Project editor: Kierra Sondereker
Managing editor: Claire Chun
Editor: Susan Lang
Proofreader: Barbara Schultz
Layout: what!design @ whatweb.com
Cocktail photographs: © Greg McBoat
Artwork from shutterstock.com: cover cocktails illustration © DiViArt; cover background pattern © RODINA OLENA; cover border Andreka_1; gold foil © Allgusak; page 6 © Igisheva Maria; pages 8, 9, 10, 13 © Babich Alexander; page 14 © Pixel-Shot; pages 42, 98 © Rimma Bondarenko; page 70 © stockcreations

To Epo and Bex, who were beside me every step of the way, and to Sean for helping me think through flavor profiles and techniques. I love you guys.

CONTENTS

INTRODUCTION

This book is a true passion project for me. When I first walked into the bright and vibrant aisles of Trader Joe's back in the 1990s, I was transfixed by products I had never heard of or only read about that Trader Joe's curated from across the globe. And it was so affordable! I was sold. Sadly for me, it would be well over a decade before TJ's would launch in my state of Colorado. Since then, my family has accepted my obsessive trips to Trader Joe's, where it can take me over an hour to explore the small store and check out everything, despite having looked up all the new products ahead of time. It was that same excitement and intrigue that led me to develop this book.

Mixology has changed significantly over the past few decades. From fresh global ingredients to science-driven technique, the cocktail world is more varied and livelier than ever. However, keeping up can be intimidating. Let this book be your guide—its seasonal groupings of 52 recipes cover 12 major classifications of cocktails:

1. Martinis: Sophisticated, traditionally made with gin or vodka, for example, the Aviation Martini (page 77)

2. Sours: Citrus as a base balanced with sweeter liquors; for example, the margarita

3. Original cocktails: Classics, such as the old-fashioned

4. Punches: Large-format drinks served in bowls and perfect for groups, such as eggnog

5. Sparklers: Drinks that incorporate sparkling soda, sparkling water, or sparkling wine, such as the mojito

6. Dessert cocktails: Sweet drinks to finish a meal, for example, the espresso martini

7. **Duos and trios**: Classic combos of spirits and liqueurs, such as the White Russian

8. **Spirit-forward cocktails**: like Originals, the classic mixed drinks, but with aromatics added, as in the Manhattan

9. **Regional drinks**: International and local drinks, such as the caipirinha, Brazil's national drink

10. **Party drinks and shots**: Fun and colorful drinks, such as tiki cocktails

11. **Morning beverages**: Classics for brunch, such as the Bloody Mary

12. **Mocktails**: Nonalcoholic drinks with complex flavors; for example, the Grapefruit Sunset (page 40)

Sure, you can follow the recipes exactly, but this book is really a guide to help you make all kinds of cocktails, from the simplest two-ingredient shot to a margarita clarified with agar-agar powder. It's for everyone who wants to become a better mixologist and party-thrower as well as anyone who just wants to nail a straightforward classic each and every time.

BARWARE

THE SHAKER

The two most common types of cocktail shakers either include a strainer or do not. My favorite is the Boston, a two-piece system with a metal shaking cup and a separate glass (usually a traditional pint glass) or metal top. The Boston allows you to shake vigorously and, with the clear pint glass, to see what you are making. You can slowly open the Boston's two containers after mixing to strain large pieces of ice and ingredients.

LEFT TO RIGHT: BOSTON AND COBBLER SHAKERS

The Cobbler shaker is what you generally get when you buy a bar kit. This shaker has a metal cup and a lid with a built-in strainer. Although this shaker works well, it does not give you as much power and control as the Boston.

STRAINERS

The key to creating clear and vibrant cocktails is the use of strainers. There are several you will use in this book. When shaking with a Boston shaker, there is no build-in strainer, so a Hawthorn strainer (with its semicircular coil on the bottom) or another fine-mesh strainer is essential. Cocktails with solids in them require a double strain using a Hawthorn or built-in shaker to catch big ice poured through a fine-mesh sieve to remove small particles. For clarified drinks, using

HAWTHORN STRAINER

cheesecloth is needed. This fine cloth is usually doubled or quadrupled and allows liquids to drain very slowly, preserving clarity and flavor.

JIGGERS

There are numerous jiggers on the market (Stepped, Japanese, and Canterbury, to name a few). Basically it is a single or double opening measuring cup. A double-sided Japanese jigger is our go-to measure of choice (with a 1-ounce and 2-ounce side). When using a jigger, hold it between your index and middle finger over your glass. Pour the liquid until it is full at the top and dump into the glass.

JAPANESE JIGGER

THE GLASSWARE

Barware is an essential step in your mixology journey. A cocktail is 50 percent taste, 30 percent appearance, and 20 percent aroma. Each drink has a recommended serving vessel, but you are welcome to use whatever works for you and highlights the story you want to tell with the drink. If you want to enjoy the aroma, try a coupe glass. To keep your drink cool and provide drama, opt for a tall, slim Collins glass. Whatever the glass, make sure to thoroughly chill it with ice water before you pour in a cold cocktail.

COLLINS   HIGHBALL   OLD-FASHIONED   ROCKS   SHOT

RED WINE GLASS   WHITE WINE GLASS   HURRICANE GLASS   COUPE GLASS   COCKTAIL/MARTINI

IRISH COFFEE GLASS   ABSINTHE GLASS   POUSSE-CAFÉ   WHISKEY SOUR   SNIFTER

OTHER EQUIPMENT

CITRUS PEELERS AND JUICERS: Citrus peelers and juicers are important when adding acid to drinks. Peelers allow you to shave pieces of zest without the bitter white pith underneath. A Mexican hand squeezer gives you maximum juice with minimal effort and cost.

SMOKING GUN: Used to add cold smoke to drinks, these tools are just a small chamber you fill with tiny wood chips, tea, or spices and a build in fan that pushes the smoke out a tube and into your cocktail. If you don't have access to a cold smoking gun, you can substitute for a drop of liquid smoke, but be careful, the flavor profile is much stronger.

SIMPLE SYRUP

Trying to mix sugar crystals into a cold drink can be nearly impossible, and thus humans created simple syrup. This 50/50 mix of sugar and water is perfect for adding sweetness to any cocktail. To make the syrup, add equal parts of sugar and water (½ cup of each) to a saucepan. Bring to a boil until all the sugar has dissolved, then remove from the heat. Simple syrup will keep for up to 1 month in the refrigerator.

This syrup serves as a blank canvas, absorbing both aromas and flavors from your favorite ingredients. Steep herbs, citrus, coffees and teas, and more in the syrup to add depth and dimension to your drinks. To make an infused syrup, add flavorings to the sugar and water. Once the mixture comes to the boil, reduce to medium-low and simmer for 5 minutes. Remove from the heat, let cool, and strain out the solids. The sky's the limit on the flavors you can create.

GARNISH 101

There are more ways to garnish your drinks than there are frozen meals at Trader Joe's. Many drinks utilize citrus peel as garnish. Here are two basic citrus garnishes every good home mixologist should know. Remember, when working with citrus peel, do your best to cut only the colorful zest and as little white pith as possible.

TWIST: Hold the citrus fruit in your hand and using a peeler or very sharp paring knife, cut along the long side of the fruit. Once you have a large, oblong piece of zest, pinch it between your thumb and forefinger to squirt the citrus oil over your drink. Drop the zest into the drink.

SPIRAL: Cut a twist with very little pith. Using a sharp paring knife, cut a long, thin strip from the twist, then tightly spiral that strip on a chopstick, pressing firmly for 30 seconds. The zest will keep a spiral shape when you release it from the chopstick.

NOTES ON ICE

We live in an age of ice enlightenment. Home mixologists can now make their own clear ice, mold ice into different shapes, and even monogram ice cubes. There are times you may want to splurge on a large ice mold for an old-fashioned so it will melt more slowly, and sometimes you may want to take a hammer to a ziplock bag of ice to create tiny shards for a tropical drink. Some recipes will include recommendations for the type of ice to best accompany the drink, but like everything in mixology, use what you have and like.

SHAKEN OR STIRRED?

In general, there are three ways to mix a drink: a dry shake, a regular shake, or to stir.

DRY SHAKE: Shaking ingredients in your shaker without ice allows them to homogenize before a regular shake.

REGULAR SHAKE: This is the classic image of Tom Cruise rocking out in the 1980s, wildly gyrating and shaking his shaker for all he's worth. There's a reason for all that gusto. Shaking does five things: it cools the drink, it mixes the drink, it incorporates air, it adds water to slightly dilute the drink, and, if you're doing it right, it breaks off tiny shards of ice for a pleasant mouthfeel. You'll want to shake when working with nonspirit beverages such as juices, milk, and coffee. Fill your shaker three-quarters full of ice, add the other ingredients, push an inverted pint glass over the shaker until it seals (you will feel the suction). Now go to town. Hold both ends of the shaker in your hands, position the shaker toward your chest, and shake as vigorously as you can, usually for between 15 and 25 seconds depending on the drink.

STIR: When you want to cool down a drink without diluting or jostling it, stir the ingredients. Stirring is usually done with spirit-only cocktails, like the Manhattan. James Bond went against the grain by shaking rather than stirring his classic martinis, but you should always stir a martini.

Remember, being a bartender or mixologist isn't just about what's in the glass. It is theater and art. So when you are shaking, make it fun, funky, and, most importantly, your own.

MUDDLING FOR FLAVOR

Muddling—mashing or crushing fruits, herbs, and spices to release their juices or oils—is a good way to add fresh flavors to a drink. You can use a tool called a muddler, which looks like a tiny baseball bat with a meat tenderizer on one end, or you can mash with a wooden spoon. Be sure to use a sturdy glass or container when muddling.

MUDDLER

SUBBING OUT INGREDIENTS?

Mixology is all about creativity and fun, so fly free with the recommendations for these recipes. If you don't like thyme, use another herb you enjoy in our Gimlet recipe.

Be aware, Trader Joe's has amazing products, but they rotate often. When this book was written in early 2024, the Trader Joe's liquors and products used in this book were available. So, if you are ready to make a Sgroppino and Trader Joe's doesn't have Calamansi and Mango Sorbet available at the moment, just use whatever sorbet you can find and enjoy.

SPRING

Honeydew Cucumber Martini

JUICES
½ cup peeled and chopped honeydew melon

½ cup peeled, seeded, and chopped cucumber

½ cup water, divided

COCKTAIL
¼ cup sugar

½ ounce fresh lemon juice

2 ounces Trader Joe's TX Vodka

1 ounce St-Germain elderflower liqueur

YIELD: 1 drink plus additional juices

What better way to kick off a cocktail book—and spring—than with a classic cocktail showcasing some of Trader Joe's great produce. Combine light and refreshing cucumber with slightly sweet honeydew for a perfect libation full of bright flavors and invigorating aromas.

1. To make the juices: Cut the honeydew and cucumber separately into rough pieces, reserving several pieces of each fruit to cube for a garnish. Blend each fruit separately with up to ¼ cup of water (if needed to help it start to blend). Strain and refrigerate.

2. To make the cocktail: Toss the cubed honeydew and cucumber in the sugar, then place the cubes on a cocktail skewer. Do this right before you mix the cocktail, so the sugar doesn't melt.

3. To a shaker filled three-quarters with ice, add ½ ounce of fresh honeydew juice and ½ ounce of fresh cucumber juice along with the lemon juice, vodka, and elderflower liqueur. Shake vigorously for 15 to 25 seconds.

4. Strain into a martini glass and garnish with the skewer of sugared fruit.

Crystal Margarita

CLARIFIED LIME JUICE

2 grams agar-agar powder

2 ounces water

8 ounces lime juice (about 8 limes)

COCKTAIL

2 ounces Trader Joe's Tequila Blanco

1 ounce triple sec

pinch of kosher salt

lime twist, for garnish

YIELD: 1 drink plus additional clear lime juice

Stripping away the frills, this recipe pays homage to the timeless margarita, letting the pure essence of quality ingredients shine. With a history dating back to the 1930s and a lineage steeped in Mexican culture, this clear rendition honors the cocktail's humble origins while offering a refreshing twist on tradition. The key is clarified lime juice. The simple technique described here creates a clean, stable juice and a crystal clear cocktail.

1. To make the clarified lime juice: Whisk the agar-agar powder into the water (ratio of 2 percent powder to liquid) and let sit while you juice the limes. Agar-agar is a thickening agent easily available online. After the thickener is added to the juice and the mixture is cooled and strained, the juice solids can be removed leaving a clear, stable juice.

2. Peel a strip of lime zest for a garnish, then juice the limes and strain. Let sit for about 5 minutes.

3. Pour the agar-agar mixture into a small saucepan and heat over medium-high to a near boil. Add the lime juice to the agar-agar mixture (not the other way around). Reduce to medium-low and cook for 5 minutes.

4. Pour the juice into a bowl and place in the refrigerator to set, about 30 minutes. It should be a loose gel, similar to aloe. It should not be solid like gelatin; if it is, you used too much agar-agar.

5. Gently break up the gel with a whisk and pour into a strainer lined with cheesecloth. Clear juice should begin to flow. If needed, gently press down on the gel with a spoon to extract the juice.

6. To make the cocktail: Fill a mixing glass ¾ full with ice, then the tequila, triple sec, salt, and clarified lime juice. Stir for 20 to 30 seconds to chill the glass (to preserve its clarity, this margarita is not shaken). Garnish with a lime twist.

The OG Sazerac

¼ ounce absinthe

1 sugar cube

3 dashes Trader Joe's Classic Bitters

2 ounces rye whiskey

1 piece of lemon peel, for garnish

YIELD: 1 drink

Classic cocktails are classic for a reason and the Sazerac, whose history dates back to the mid-1800s, is the grandpappy of them all. This recipe is all about the rye whiskey with some simple accoutrements—absinthe, sugar, bitters, and lemon—to make it shine. If you really want to showcase great spirits and technique, break out a Sazerac and impress your friends.

1. Add the absinthe to a chilled rocks glass, and swirl to coat the inside of the glass. Pour out any excess.

2. Place the sugar cube and bitters in a mixing glass. Muddle to break up the sugar cube. Add the whiskey, then fill the glass halfway with ice. Stir for 20 to 30 seconds.

3. Hold the lemon twist between your thumb and forefinger and squeeze the oils over the drink. Drop the peel into the drink.

Grilled Pineapple Sangria

¼ cup sugar

1 teaspoon Chinese five spice powder

½ pineapple, horizontal section, peeled and sliced into ½-inch rounds

½ cup unpeeled and chopped orange

¼ cup unpeeled and chopped lime

1 lemon, unpeeled and chopped

2 large sprigs of fresh mint, chopped

2 (750-ml) bottles sauvignon blanc

2 cups Trader Joe's Cold Pressed Pineapple Juice

½ cup Trader Joe's White Rum of the Gods

2 cups Trader Joe's Sparkling Lemon Water

⟿⟽

YIELD: 12 drinks

Inspired by the sun-soaked vineyards of Spain, sangria has long been a staple of warm-weather celebrations. This version puts a twist on tradition by infusing the classic concoction with the smoky sweetness of grilled pineapple, creating a symphony of flavors that dance on the palate.

1. Mix the sugar with the Chinese five spice powder. Toss the rounds of pineapple in the spiced sugar. Place on a preheated grill or grill pan on medium-high heat, and cook until caramelized on both sides. Remove and let cool.

2. Once the grilled pineapple is cool, chop 2 rounds into strips.

3. Place the chopped pineapple, orange, lime, lemon, and mint into a pitcher and muddle with a wooden spoon or muddler.

4. Pour the wine, pineapple juice, and rum into the pitcher, and stir. Refrigerate for at least 30 minutes, but an hour would be better.

5. When you are ready to serve, strain the mixture to remove the solid fruit.

6. Add the sparkling water and stir lightly.

7. Serve in cocktail glasses, with a cut slice of grilled pineapple in each.

Mint Mojito with Manuka Honey

HONEY-MINT SYRUP

1 cup fresh lime juice

¾ cup manuka honey

5 large sprigs of fresh mint, chopped, divided

COCKTAIL

½ lime, cut into wedges

1½ ounces Trader Joe's White Rum of the Gods

1 can Trader Joe's Plain Sparkling Water

YIELD: 1 drink plus additional syrup

One of the best things about TJ's is your ability to have luxury on a budget. Originating in Cuba in the 16th century, the mojito has remained a beloved cocktail thanks to its invigorating blend of rum, mint, and lime. Manuka honey, a prized ingredient known for its rich flavor and health benefits, elevates this timeless drink to new heights.

1. To make the honey-mint syrup: Add the lime juice, honey, and 4 of the mint sprigs to a small saucepan over medium heat. Simmer for 5 minutes, then remove from the heat. Strain the mixture and refrigerate.

2. To make the cocktail: Add the remaining mint sprig, the lime, and 1 ounce of the honey-mint syrup to a Collins glass. Muddle the ingredients gently.

3. Fill the glass halfway with ice, add the rum and top with soda water. Stir lightly.

Spicy Espresso Mezcal Martini

SPICED SUGAR

1 tablespoon turbinado raw cane sugar

½ teaspoon cinnamon

¼ teaspoon chipotle powder

¼ teaspoon ground cloves

COCKTAIL

2 ounces Espada Pequeña Mezcal

1 ounce brewed and chilled Trader Joe's Shade Grown Ground Espresso Blend

1 ounce heavy cream

coffee beans, for garnish

YIELD: 1 drink plus additional spiced sugar

The espresso martini is certainly having a moment, so here's an easy way to spice things up! This recipe adds a twist with the addition of mezcal, a complex spirit with roots in ancient Nahuatl tradition, creating a drink that is rich, smoky, and spicy.

1. To make the spiced sugar: In a small bowl, stir together the sugar, cinnamon, chipotle powder, and ground cloves with a spoon.

2. To make the cocktail: To a shaker, add 1 tablespoon of the spiced sugar along with the mezcal, espresso, and heavy cream. Shake vigorously for 20 to 30 seconds (a bit more than usual to thoroughly combine the sugar and froth the cream).

3. Strain into a martini glass. Top half of the drink with the spiced sugar and garnish the other half with coffee beans.

Thyme Gimlet

THYME SYRUP
1 cup sugar

1 cup water

7 sprigs of fresh thyme, divided

COCKTAIL
2½ ounces Trader Joe's Art of the Still Organic Gin

½ ounce fresh lime juice

YIELD: 1 drink plus additional syrup

The gimlet is the classic cocktail created by the British Royal Navy in the 19th century to fight scurvy and what... sobriety? It's the quintessential expression of lightness and spring, so why not build on the herbal notes of the gin? This rendition adds a modern twist with the infusion of fragrant thyme into simple syrup, a refreshing tribute to the timeless allure of botanical-infused libations.

1. To make the thyme syrup: Add the sugar, water, and 6 of the thyme sprigs to a small saucepan. Bring to a boil, then immediately reduce to medium-low and simmer for 10 minutes. Strain out the thyme and refrigerate the syrup.

2. To make the cocktail: Fill a shaker three-quarters full with ice, then add the gin, lime juice, and ½ ounce of the thyme syrup. Shake vigorously for 15 to 25 seconds.

3. Strain into a chilled cocktail glass and garnish with the remaining thyme sprig.

Sour Cherry Foam Martinez

SOUR CHERRY FOAM

1 cup Trader Joe's 100% Red Tart Cherry Juice

1¾ ounces fresh lemon juice

1½ grams soy lecithin powder

COCKTAIL

2 ounces Trader Joe's Art of the Still Organic Gin

1 ounce sweet vermouth

¼ ounce Luxardo maraschino liqueur

5 dashes Trader Joe's Classic Bitters

YIELD: 1 drink plus additional foam

Among the most distinctive historical drinks, the Martinez links the old-fashioned and the modern martini. Dating back to the 1880s, the Martinez boasts a rich history of refinement and sophistication and is often hailed as the predecessor to the modern martini. This is a great example of how you can easily use some basic science to up your mixology game by creating a stable foam, in this case, a luxurious cherry foam, that adds flavor and texture.

1. To make the sour cherry foam: To a large bowl, add the cherry and lemon juices and the soy lecithin powder (easily available online). The soy lecithin is essential for stabilizing the foam and allowing liquids to make and maintain bubbles more easily. Usually, you add ½ percent by weight of soy lecithin to liquid.

2. Using an immersion blender, blend the juices and soy lecithin for about 60 seconds. For more bubbles, agitate or rapidly move the blender and try to incorporate as much air as possible. A foam will form on the top of the juices. It should be stable for at least 30 minutes, so blend only when you're ready to make the cocktail.

3. To make the cocktail: Add the gin, sweet vermouth, maraschino liqueur, and bitters to a mixing glass filled halfway with ice, and stir until well chilled, about 30 seconds.

4. Strain into a chilled coupe glass, and top with a line of cherry foam.

Caipirinha with Lime

1 lime, cut into wedges

2 teaspoons Trader Joe's Turbinado Raw Cane Sugar

2 ounces cachaça

lime wheels, for garnish

YIELD: 1 drink

It isn't possible to create a Trader Joe's cocktail book without some major globe-trotting. Luckily, we now have better access to ingredients and products from across the world. One of the best drinks comes from the sun-drenched beaches of Brazil: the caipirinha. A refreshing concoction dating back to the 19th century, the caipirinha is Brazil's national cocktail, featuring the distinctive flavor of cachaça (a Brazilian liquor distilled from sugarcane), fresh lime, and sugar.

1. In a rocks glass, muddle the lime wedges and sugar until the sugar dissolves.

2. Fill the glass with ice and add the cachaça.

3. Stir to incorporate all the ingredients and garnish with wheels of lime.

Jalapeño Limeade Gelatin Shot

3 large limes

2 serrano chilis

1¼ cup Trader Joe's Organic Jalapeño Limeade, divided

1 (3-ounce) package gelatin

¼ cup fresh lime juice

½ cup Espada Pequeña Mezcal

sea salt

YIELD: Approximately 40 gelatin shots

Sure, a gelatin shot may be a callback to trashy house parties and hangovers, and there is nothing wrong with that—but here is an adult version with a fiery fusion of flavors that packs a punch. Inspired by the traditional Mexican spirit of mezcal, this bold concoction combines the smoky notes of mezcal with the zesty tang of lime and the fiery kick of jalapeño. Complex flavors, and the use of fresh produce as the shot vessels, elevates this party shot into spicy specialness.

1. Slice the limes lengthwise into halves. Remove the fruit with a spoon, being careful to leave the pith and zest. Juice the fruit and reserve the hollow lime halves.

2. Slice the serranos lengthwise into halves and remove all the seeds and white ribs. Set aside the hollow chili halves.

3. In a small saucepan, heat 1 cup of the jalapeño limeade to a near boil. Add the gelatin and stir for 2 minutes until completely dissolved. Remove from the heat, and pour into a large, heat-safe measuring cup.

4. Pour in the remaining ¼ cup of cold limeade and the fresh lime juice to cool down the mixture. Add the mezcal and stir. Allow to cool at room temperature for about 10 minutes.

5. Place the hollow lime and serrano chili halves on a tray lined with a kitchen towel so the fruits remain stable. Carefully pour the gelatin mixture into them.

6. Place the tray in the refrigerator and allow the gelatin to solidify following package directions, usually 4 to 6 hours.

7. Once the contents are solid, remove and slice into quarters. Serve with salt.

Tropical Mimosa

¾ cup Trader Joe's
Platinum Reserve
Brut Sparkling Wine
Sonoma County

¼ cup Trader Joe's
Orange Peach
Mango Juice

Trader Joe's Sweetened
Green Mango,
for garnish

YIELD: 1 drink

Raise a glass to the classic brunch companion, the mimosa. With its origins tracing back to 1920s Paris, this effervescent cocktail has remained a symbol of indulgence and celebration. With one stop at Trader Joe's you will have all the ingredients to turn the brunch staple into a tropical treat using mango two ways.

1. Add the sparkling wine to a fluted glass.

2. Slowly pour in the mango juice.

3. Slice a notch in a piece of dried mango and place it on the rim of the glass as a tasty garnish.

Vegan Yuzu Flip (Mocktail)

½ ounce simple syrup
(page 11)

½ ounce fresh lemon juice

1 ounce Trader Joe's
Coconut Cream

2 ounces Trader Joe's
Sparkling Coconut
Water with Yuzu

YIELD: 1 drink

Flips, which have been around for more than three centuries, usually feature a foamy top made with eggs. This mocktail uses sparkling water and coconut cream to make a vegan version that highlights the unique East Asian citrus, yuzu (tasting somewhat like a more fragrant lemon).

1. To a shaker, add the simple syrup, lemon juice, and coconut cream, and shake without ice for 10 to 15 seconds.

2. Open the shaker and fill three-quarters full with ice. Shake a second time for 20 to 30 seconds.

3. Strain into a coupe glass, and top with the sparkling coconut water.

Grapefruit Sunset (Mocktail)

HIBISCUS SYRUP

½ cup water

½ cup sugar

¼ cup dried
hibiscus flowers

2 cinnamon sticks

½ inch knob of
fresh ginger

MOCKTAIL

½ cup Trader Joe's
Grapefruit Juice

¼ cup Trader Joe's
Sparkling Grapefruit
Spring Water

YIELD: 1 drink

Inspired by the tequila sunset and Trader Joe's Dried Sweetened Hibiscus Flowers, this mocktail lightens up a traditionally overly sweet drink by substituting hibiscus syrup for grenadine. It also uses grapefruit juice and soda to give a slight effervescence sparkle.

1. To make the hibiscus syrup: Add the sugar, water, hibiscus flowers, cinnamon, and ginger to a small saucepan. Bring to a boil over medium-high heat, then reduce to medium-low and simmer for 15 minutes.

2. Remove from the heat and allow to steep at room temperature for another 30 to 60 minutes. Strain out the hibiscus flowers (you can roll the syrup-drenched flowers in more sugar for a tasty treat).

3. To make the mocktail: Fill a chilled glass with grapefruit juice, and top with the sparkling water. Slowly pour in 1 ounce of the hibiscus syrup to create a beautiful sunset layer in the glass.

SUMMER

Fleur de Paradis

2 ounces Trader Joe's Art of the Still Organic Gin

1 ounce St-Germain elderflower liqueur

½ ounce fresh grapefruit juice

½ ounce fresh lemon juice

1 dash orange bitters

1 to 3 ounces Trader Joe's Platinum Reserve Brut Sparkling Sonoma County, chilled

edible flowers, for garnish

YIELD: 1 drink

Sometimes a person just needs to get the fancy out, and this is the cocktail to make you feel lux and light. Named for the rare and exotic flower, this cocktail combines delicate floral notes with the crispness of quality spirits, creating a drink that is as elegant as it is enchanting. With its subtle complexity and refined flavors, it's the perfect libation for those who appreciate the finer things in life or at least pretend to.

1. To a shaker three-quarters filled with ice, add the gin, elderflower liqueur, juices, and bitters.

2. Shake for 15 to 25 seconds and double-strain into a coupe glass.

3. Top with the sparkling wine, and garnish with edible flowers.

My Paloma

1 tablespoon Trader Joe's Pink Salt Crystals

1 lime, for zest, juice, and garnish

2 ounces Trader Joe's Tequila Blanco

4 ounces Villa Italia Italian Grapefruit Soda

YIELD: 1 drink

One of the most classic of all summer sour drinks is the paloma. As classic as it is simple, this cocktail gets extra zip from a lime zest and pink salt rim. If you want something not overly sweet for a hot day, try M-m-m-my Paloma.

1. Place the salt on a small plate, and grate half of the lime zest directly over the salt.

2. Cut the lime in half. Slice a thin wheel from one half for a garnish. Juice one of the halves onto a second small plate and juice the other half into a small cup.

3. To rim the glass in salt, invert a tall Collins glass and place the rim first into the plate of lime juice. Spin it around lightly to ensure the juice coats the rim. Allow any excess juice to drip off the glass. Place the rim into the plate of salt and lime zest. Remove and let dry for a minute. Fill with ice cubes.

4. To make the cocktail, add the tequila, grapefruit soda, and lime juice to the rimmed glass and stir for 15 to 20 seconds.

5. Cut a notch into the lime wheel and place on the rim of the glass.

Smoked Clementine Mezcal Milk Punch

2 bags Trader Joe's Organic Blood Orange Rooibos Herbal Tea Blend

5 clementines, unpeeled and roughly chopped, divided

½ cup dark brown sugar

½ teaspoon salt

¼ teaspoon ground chipotle

¼ teaspoon ground cloves

1½ cups Trader Joe's Cold Pressed Orange Juice

4 ounces Espada Pequeña Mezcal

4 ounces brandy

¼ cup fresh lemon juice

1 cup whole milk

YIELD: 4 drinks

Despite the name, milk punch is not a creamy, eggnogg-esque holiday drink. It has long been a favorite among cocktail enthusiasts thanks to its silky texture and luxurious taste. This is achieved by using the reaction between acids and milk to remove impurities, clarify the drink, add sweetness, and create a more well-rounded mouthfeel. In this version of milk punch, mezcal and smoking add increased complexity.

1. Brew 2 tea bags in 8 ounces of water. Set aside to cool.

2. To a pitcher add 4 of the chopped clementines along with the brown sugar, salt, chipotle, and cloves, and crush with a muddler or wooden spoon until well combined, 30 to 60 seconds. The more you muddle, the more oils will be released from the clementine rinds.

3. Add the orange juice, mezcal, brandy, lemon juice, and cooled tea to the pitcher. Let sit at room temperature for 30 minutes, then strain.

4. Pour the milk into a pitcher or other suitable container. Add the strained juice and liquor mixture and mix with a spoon. Do not add the milk to the juice and liquor mixture or the milk will coagulate too quickly. Let sit at room temperature for 30 minutes.

5. Slowly pour the mixture into a strainer lined with 4 layers of cheesecloth and set over a bowl or pitcher. Let gravity filter the mixture; do not press on it. The liquid should filter through within 15 minutes.

6. Chill the clear liquid in the refrigerator.

7. To make each drink, add 4 to 6 ounces (depending on your punch glass) of punch to a mixing glass and stir for 30 seconds. Pour into the punch glasses, making sure to leave at least one-half to one-quarter of the glass empty.

8. Following the instructions for using a cold smoking gun, smoke the top of the punch and drink immediately.

The Algonquin

1½ ounces rye whiskey

¾ ounce dry vermouth

¾ ounce Trader Joe's Cold Pressed Pineapple Juice

YIELD: 1 drink

Named for the iconic New York City hotel where it was first served in the 1930s, the Algonquin cocktail exudes style and glamor. It features fresh pineapple juice. Even for mixologists, making fresh juice is always time-consuming, so Trader Joe's comes to the rescue with an amazing selection of fresh juices, including pineapple, you can use to easily make tasty cocktails.

1. Pour all the ingredients into a shaker three-quarters filled with ice.

2. Shake vigorously for 15 to 25 seconds, then strain into a chilled coupe glass.

Calamansi Sgroppino

3 tablespoons Trader Joe's Calamansi and Mango Sorbet

½ ounce Trader Joe's TX Vodka

1 ounce Trader Joe's Prosecco

YIELD: 1 drink

Named for the Venetian tradition of mixing sorbet with sparkling wine, this cocktail exudes old-world charm and timeless elegance. It utilizes calamansi, a Filipino citrus fruit with a sour kick. Trader Joe's Calamansi and Mango Sorbet is a tour of flavors across Europe and Asia. Remember, TJ's switches out products, so use any seasonal sorbet on offer.

1. Scoop the sorbet into a coupe glass.

2. Pour the vodka over the sorbet, then add the prosecco.

Sparkling Strawberry Ranch Water

2 strawberries, for garnish

1 lime, for juice and garnish

2 ounces Trader Joe's Tequila Blanco

4 ounces Trader Joe's Sparkling Strawberry Juice Beverage

YIELD: 1 drink

Inspired by the natural beauty of the Texas Hill Country, ranch water has become a beloved cocktail thanks to its crisp and invigorating flavors. The only thing better than the refreshing coldness of classic ranch water is this version featuring fresh summer strawberries to marry with the sweetness of young, blanco tequila.

1. Slice the strawberries into rounds.

2. Slice the lime in half. Juice half and cut the other into rounds.

3. Fill a Collins glass with ice. Pour in the tequila, sparkling juice, and lime juice, and stir lightly.

4. Garnish with the lime and strawberry rounds.

Fresh Grasshopper

3 sprigs of fresh mint, divided

1 tablespoon Trader Joe's Organic Midnight Moo Chocolate Syrup

2 ounces heavy cream

1½ ounces white crème de cacao

1½ ounces crème de menthe

Trader Joe's Pound Plus 72% Cacao Dark Chocolate Bar, for garnish

YIELD: 1 drink

Yes, the grasshopper used to be the favorite of octogenarian barflies, but it is becoming more and more in vogue. By relying on some prepared Trader Joe's ingredients along with lighter and fresher versions of the classic contents, you can transform this cocktail into a delectable summer sipper.

1. Add 2 sprigs of the mint along with the chocolate syrup and the heavy cream to a shaker. Using a muddler or wooden spoon, crush the mint into the syrup and heavy cream for 15 seconds.

2. Add enough ice to fill the shake three-quarters full, then add the two liqueurs. Shake vigorously for 15 to 25 seconds. Double-strain into a martini or punch glass.

3. Using your hand, warm one side of the bar of chocolate slightly (this will make for much better curls). With a vegetable peeler, make curls by slowly and firmly scraping down the warmed edge of the chocolate.

4. Garnish with shaved chocolate and the remaining mint sprig.

Basil Julep

BASIL-MINT SYRUP

2 cups water

2 cups sugar

½ cup chopped fresh basil leaves

¼ cup chopped fresh mint leaves

¼ teaspoon salt

COCKTAIL

1½ cups crushed ice, or as needed

4 ounces Trader Joe's Kentucky Bourbon Straight Whiskey

fresh basil leaves, for garnish

YIELD: 1 drink plus additional syrup

An iconic American cocktail and a staple of the Kentucky Derby since the late 19th century, the julep is filled with icy sweetness and bourbon that can sneak up on you. The classic mint cocktail is great, but this version calls for adding basil leaves, at peak in summer, for an irresistible earthiness.

1. To make the basil-mint syrup: In a small saucepan, bring the water, sugar, chopped basil and mint, and salt to a boil over high heat, then reduce to medium-low. Cook for 5 more minutes, remove from the heat, and allow to come to room temperature to further infuse the herbs. Strain the syrup and refrigerate.

2. To make the cocktail: Fill a julep cup with crushed ice, then pour in the bourbon and 2 ounces of the basil-mint syrup.

3. Garnish with torn basil leaves.

Sumo Aperol Spritz

1 Sumo mandarin, sliced into rounds, for garnish

3 ounces Trader Joe's Prosecco

2 ounces Aperol

1 ounce Trader Joe's Cranberry Clementine Sparkling Water

YIELD: 1 drink

On a patio enjoying a sunset, at an afternoon barbecue, at the scorching beach, or on a first date because you want to look cool but don't like bitter drinks—anytime is time for an Aperol spritz. Originating in Venice in the early 20th century, the Aperol spritz has become a beloved aperitif thanks to its vibrant color and bittersweet flavor.

1. Fill a large wine glass with ice and several slices of Sumo mandarin.

2. Add the prosecco, Aperol, and sparkling water. Stir briefly.

Electric Blue Lemonade

¾ ounce Trader Joe's TX Vodka

½ ounce fresh lemon juice

¾ ounce Trader Joe's Limoncello Sicilian Liqueur

½ ounce blue curaçao

12 ounces Trader Joe's Fresh Squeezed Lemonade

⅓ cup Trader Joe's Blueberry Lemonade Sparkling Water

YIELD: 1 drink

A true party drink requires breaking out some fun-colored spirits to encapsulate the vibrant energy of city nightlife and the playful spirit of summer festivals. Enter blue curaçao, a sweet, orange-flavored liqueur with the most vibrant azure hue. If you enjoy a good hard lemonade, this is the drink for you.

1. Pour the vodka, lemon juice, limoncello, blue curaçao, and lemonade into a shaker filled three-quarters full of ice. Shake vigorously for 15 to 25 seconds.

2. Pour into a pint glass with filled with ice, and top with sparkling water.

Chili Bloody Mary with a Charcuterie Skewer

2 tablespoons Trader Joe's Crunchy Chili Onion, divided

Trader Joe's Bloody Mary Mixer with Clam Juice

2 ounces Trader Joe's TX Vodka

1 lime, for juice and garnish

1 ounce Trader Joe's Unexpected Cheddar Cheese

1 ounce Trader Joe's Ubriaco al Cabernet

2 slices Trader Joe's Uncured Salame di Parma Mild Salami

1 Trader Joe's Grilled Pitted Green Olive

YIELD: 1 drink

Who doesn't like a charcuterie board? Why not put the fixings on a skewer and use it to top an extra-spicy Bloody Mary? The ingredients listed here include a selection of Trader Joe's cheeses, salami, and olives—but given the amazing selection available, use your imagination and choose what appeals to you. Rim with Trader Joe's Crunchy Chili Onion for extra tang.

1. Place 1 tablespoon of the Crunchy Chili Onion on a small plate.

2. Invert a pint mason jar and rim it in the dip.

3. Fill ¾ full with ice and add the remaining 1 tablespoon of the chili onion dip, and the Bloody Mary mix, vodka, and juice of half the lime. Stir.

4. Thread all the best items from a charcuterie board plus a lime wedge on a long toothpick or skewer and lay it across the mouth of the jar.

Mango Slushy Boba (Mocktail)

1 pouch Trader Joe's Instant Boba Kit

½ cup Trader Joe's Mango Chunks, frozen

4 ounces Trader Joe's 100% Mango Juice

1 ounce fresh lime juice

YIELD: 1 drink

Just a few years ago, bubble tea could be found only in Asian neighborhoods and restaurants. Now it is almost as common as Starbucks coffee. Bubble tea is any drink with fruit, tea, or dairy, usually but not always paired with chewy, sweet tapioca pearls called boba. Though there is technique and specific ingredients to make these gummy gems, Trader Joe's has a frozen boba kit containing tapioca pearls flavored with rich brown sugar that partner perfectly with a sweet mango slushy.

1. Prepare the Trader Joe's boba syrup and pearls following package directions.

2. To a blender (or a tall container if using an immersion blender), add the frozen mango, mango juice, lime juice, and ½ cup ice. Blend until smooth to create a mango slushy.

3. To a pint glass, add the boba and the syrup (reserving a tablespoon to garnish the top), followed by the mango slushy. Top with some extra syrup and add a large boba straw.

Everything AND the Elote Milkshake (Mocktail)

1 cup Trader Joe's Organic Corn Flakes

3 cups Trader Joe's Organic Whole Milk from Grass Fed Cows

¼ cup Trader Joe's Organic Heavy Whipping Cream

2 tablespoons light corn syrup

¼ cup plus 2 tablespoons Trader Joe's Greek Nonfat Yogurt Plain, divided

1 teaspoon Trader Joe's Everything but the Elote Seasoning Blend plus more for garnish

¼ cup Trader Joe's Frozen Roasted Corn

1 cup Trader Joe's French Vanilla Ice Cream

grated zest of 1 lime

¼ teaspoon smoked paprika

OPTIONAL TO UN-MOCKTAIL IT

2 ounces Trader Joe's Kentucky Bourbon Straight Whiskey (add to step 3 if using)

YIELD: 2 milkshakes

Adding savory ingredients pushes this milkshake over the top for a unique summer treat. One of the most popular global flavors Trader Joe's has brought to the everyday American table is elote, the Mexican street food consisting of roasted corn on the cob typically slathered with crema, spice, lime, and cheese. Trader Joe's has re-created that flavor in Everything but the Elote Seasoning Blend, which contains all the mouthwatering ingredients minus the corn.

1. Create cornflake milk by adding the cornflakes to the milk. Mix with a spoon and refrigerate for 30 to 60 minutes. Strain out the cornflakes and keep the milk.

2. To make the whipped cream, whisk together the whipping cream and corn syrup until soft peaks form. Add ¼ cup of the yogurt and the elote seasoning, and lightly mix to combine.

3. To make the milkshakes, combine the cornflake milk, corn, ice cream, lime zest, and paprika plus the remaining 2 tablespoons of yogurt in a blender. Blend until smooth and homogenized, about 60 seconds.

4. Pour into two tall glasses, and top with the elote whipped cream, a few frozen corn kernels, and some elote seasoning.

AUTUMN

Cookie Butter Old-Fashioned

FAT-WASHED BOURBON

½ cup Trader Joe's Speculoos Cookie Butter Spread (creamy), plus more for garnish

1 (750-ml) bottle Trader Joe's Kentucky Best Bourbon Straight Whiskey

SPICED SYRUP

¼ cup dark brown sugar

¼ cup water

½ teaspoon ground cinnamon

½ teaspoon ground cloves

½ teaspoon ground cardamom

COCKTAIL

3 dashes Trader Joe's Classic Bitters

orange peel, for garnish

YIELD: 1 drink plus additional fat-washed bourbon and syrup

The savory flavor of Trader Joe's Speculoos Cookie Butter updates this simple yet sophisticated cocktail. Using cookie butter to fat-wash bourbon (adding a fatty ingredient to liquor for texture and flavor) and reinforcing those flavors with a spiced syrup imbues the classic old-fashioned with warmth and snuggly goodness.

1. To fat-wash the bourbon: In a medium saucepan over medium-low heat, warm the cookie butter until melted and runny, 5 to 10 minutes. Remove from the heat and pour the bourbon into the saucepan. Whisk to combine, 30 to 60 seconds. Leave uncovered until completely cool.

2. Freeze the mixture, skim off the solids, and then strain through cheesecloth to remove the remaining solids. The mixture may still be slightly cloudy. It will keep in the refrigerator for several months.

3. To make the spiced syrup: Add the brown sugar, water, and spices to a small saucepan, and bring to a boil. Remove from the heat when all the sugar is dissolved, and cool at room temperature. When cool, funnel into a bottle and refrigerate.

4. To make the cocktail: Add 2 ounces of the fat-washed bourbon, ½ ounce of the spiced syrup, and the bitters to a mixing glass filled with ice. Stir vigorously for 30 seconds.

5. Warm a few tablespoons of cookie butter in the microwave for 15 to 25 seconds until runny and add to a small plate. Invert a rocks glass, and rim it in the melted cookie butter. Then strain the contents of the mixing glass into the rocks glass, over a single large ice cube.

6. With a peeler or sharp paring knife, cut off a large peel from the orange, being careful to remove as little pith as possible. Squeeze the peel between your thumb and forefinger over a lit match and into the glass. Squeezing will spray out some of the orange oil and give the drink a slightly charred citrus note. Drop the peel into the drink.

Anjou Pear Punch

2 Anjou pears, divided

1 teaspoon ground cinnamon

2 cups pear juice

1 cup Trader Joe's Blended Scotch Whisky

YIELD: 4 drinks

Pumpkin spice lattes and apple cider are the typical, commonplace beverages of autumn. Go against the expected by mixing crisp pear, warming spices, and smooth scotch for a satisfying punch. Inspired by the bountiful harvests of autumn and the cozy comforts of home, this cocktail is a tribute to the simple pleasures of the season and is anything but the usual.

1. Seed and dice 1 of the Anjou pears. Add the diced pear and the cinnamon to a pitcher, and crush with a muddler or wooden spoon seconds for 30 seconds.

2. Pour in the pear juice and Scotch. Stir for 30 seconds to combine.

3. Refrigerate for at least 60 minutes, then strain out the chunks of pear.

4. Using a mandolin or very sharp knife, thinly slice the other pear lengthwise. Place a slice in each punch or rocks glass and add the punch.

Aviation Martini

2 ounces Trader Joe's Art of the Still Organic Gin

¾ ounce fresh lemon juice

½ ounce maraschino liqueur

¼ ounce crème de violette

Trader Joe's Amarena Cherries, for garnish

YIELD: 1 drink

Soar to new heights with the Aviation cocktail, a classic libation with a touch of vintage glamor. Dating back to the early 20th century, the Aviation has become a favorite of cocktail enthusiasts thanks to its delicate balance of floral gin, tart lemon juice, and aromatic maraschino liqueur. The all-star of this beautiful bevvy is crème de violette, with its amazing purple-blue color from violet flowers.

1. Combine the gin, lemon juice, and liqueurs in a cocktail shaker.

2. Fill the shaker three-quarters full with ice, and shake for 15 to 25 seconds.

3. Double-strain into a martini glass, and garnish with a cherry.

Parisian Blonde

1 ounce Trader Joe's White Rum of the Gods

1 ounce orange curaçao

1 ounce heavy cream

1 Sumo mandarin

fresh whole nutmeg

YIELD: 1 drink

Despite a name that sounds like a Eurovision finalist, this balanced drink has everything. Heavy cream and curaçao give it creamy and sweet notes, while nutmeg and mandarin provide earthy and bright tones. It's the perfect drink for toasting to romance or for rooting on your favorite Europop group.

1. Fill a shaker three-quarters full with ice, and add the rum, curaçao, and heavy cream.

2. Zest one-quarter of the rind of a Sumo mandarin into the shaker.

3. Shake for 15 to 25 seconds, then strain into a coupe glass.

4. Grate fresh nutmeg over the drink, and place a round of mandarin zest on the rim.

Ginger Whiskey Sour

GINGER SYRUP

1 (1-inch) knob of ginger

½ cup sugar

½ cup water

COCKTAIL

2 ounces Trader Joe's
Kentucky Bourbon
Straight Whiskey

¾ ounce fresh lemon juice

**YIELD: 1 drink plus
additional syrup**

*Like many original cocktails, whiskey sours orig-
inated in the 19th century and used citrus juice
and a sweetener to mask the flavor of harsh spirits.
Infusing this classic with a savory kick of fresh
ginger makes a drink that is as invigorating as it is
delicious.*

1. To make the ginger syrup: Add the ginger,
sugar, and water to a small saucepan. Bring to
a boil, then reduce to medium-low and simmer
for 5 minutes. Remove from the heat and let
cool to room temperature before straining out
the ginger and refrigerating.

2. To make the cocktail: Add 1 ounce of the
syrup plus the bourbon and lemon juice to a
shaker three-quarters filled with ice. Shake for
15 to 25 seconds, then strain into a rocks glass.

Seattle Mule

2 ounces Trader
Joe's TX Vodka

½ ounce fresh lime juice

1 ounce Trader Joe's
Sparkling Apple Cider

4 ounces Reed's
Craft Ginger Beer

sprig of fresh mint,
for garnish

YIELD: 1 drink

Embrace the spirit of the Pacific Northwest with the Seattle Mule, a refreshing twist on the classic Moscow Mule. Infused with the crisp sweetness of apple cider and the invigorating kick of ginger beer, this cocktail pays homage to the lush orchards and misty landscapes of the region. You get a taste of the Pacific Northwest in every sip, perfect for cozy evenings by the fire or lively gatherings with friends.

1. Fill a copper mug with ice.

2. Pour in the vodka, lime juice, apple cider, and ginger beer and stir slightly.

3. Garnish with a mint sprig for aroma.

Candied Orange Manhattan

2 ounces Trader Joe's Kentucky Bourbon Straight Whiskey

1 ounce sweet vermouth

2 or 3 dashes Trader Joe's Classic Bitters

Trader Joe's Trader Joe's Sweetened Dried Orange Slices, for garnish

Trader Joe's Amarena Cherries, for garnish

YIELD: 1 drink

One of the best things about Trader Joe's is its limitless supply of tasty cocktail garnishes. The Amarena cherry and sweetened orange add elegance to a sophisticated and timeless cocktail named for the iconic borough that has long been synonymous with style and class. The Manhattan remains a favorite of cocktail enthusiasts thanks to its rich flavor and smooth finish.

1. Chill a coupe glass.

2. Fill a mixing glass with ice, then add the bourbon, vermouth, and bitters. Stir well and strain into the glass.

3. Place an Amarena cherry on a slice of orange and fold the orange and cherry like a taco and skewer it with a toothpick. Set it across the glass as a garnish.

Ramos Gin Fizz

2 ounces Trader Joe's Art of the Still Organic Gin

2 ounces half-and-half

½ ounce lemon juice

½ ounce lime juice

2 teaspoons sugar

1 egg white

3 dashes orange flower water

1 dash vanilla extract

1 ounce Trader Joe's Plain Sparkling Water, or as needed

lemon zest, for garnish

YIELD: 1 drink

Originating in the late 19th century, the Ramos Gin Fizz has become a beloved favorite thanks to its frothy texture and delicate flavor profile. This unusual blend of ingredients plays off the botanical notes of the gin to create a unique cocktail that will be an important tool in your bartending arsenal. There is no need to fear the raw egg white (this is mixology and there is no room for the faint of heart), but feel free to purchase pasteurized egg whites.

1. To a shaker, add the gin, half-and-half, juices, sugar, egg white, orange flower water, and vanilla extract. Dry shake for 20 to 30 seconds to incorporate the dairy with the egg white.

2. Add ice to fill the shaker three-quarters full and shake for an additional 15 to 25 seconds to cool the drink and create foam.

3. Strain into a Collins glass, top with sparking water to fill, and garnish with lemon zest.

Earl Grey Tea Smoked Brandy Alexander

1 ounce brandy

1 ounce crème de cacao

1 ounce heavy cream

1 Trader Joe's Organic Earl Grey Tea bag

fresh whole nutmeg

YIELD: 1 drink

An Alexander drink is often cloyingly sweet and can be one note. By using the smoke from Earl Grey tea, you can accentuate this dessert cocktail with notes of fire and bergamot (the tea contains oils from Italian bergamot oranges). The smoke effect is beautiful in a snifter glass and adds complexity to the drink.

1. Fill a cocktail shaker three-quarters full of ice, and add the brandy, crème de cacao, and heavy cream. Shake for 15 to 25 seconds.

2. Strain into a snifter glass and grate fresh nutmeg over the top.

3. Using a smoking gun that can smoke using tea, cut open the Earl Grey tea bags and empty the tea into the smoker. Use as directed to fill the snifter with a light tea smoke. If you don't have a smoker, you can add 2 drops of liquid smoke to the tea.

Wake the Dead Layered Shot

½ ounce brewed and cooled Trader Joe's Shade Grown Espresso Blend

1 ounce coffee liqueur

1 ounce Trader Joe's Tequila Blanco

YIELD: 1 shot

The combination of caffeine and alcohol has been around since someone had the wise idea to mix an energy drink with vodka. Kickstart your party with this bold and spirited concoction inspired by the tradition of layered shots and the playful spirit of Halloween. This shot doubles down on coffee to enliven any fall festivity.

1. Pour the espresso into a shot glass.

2. Using the back of a small spoon, very slowly (using a pour spout if possible) pour the coffee liqueur over the espresso, creating a layer.

3. Using the same method, layer the tequila over the espresso. You should see 3 layers in the glass.

Cloudy Irish Coffee

1½ ounces Trader Joe's Kentucky Bourbon Straight Whiskey

2 teaspoons brown sugar

4 to 6 ounces brewed Joe Medium Roast Ground Coffee

3 tablespoons heavy cream

½ teaspoon Trader Joe's Bourbon Vanilla Bean Paste

YIELD: 1 drink

Irish coffee is simple and classic and, really, it's all about that mildly sweet cream topping that plays beautifully with the warming effects from the hot coffee and the intense whiskey. Do not skimp on the cream. Don't be tempted to add sugar to the cloud of cream or the drink's flavor will not be balanced.

1. Prewarm a translucent coffee cup by adding hot water and letting it sit for 1 minute before discarding the water.

2. Add the bourbon and brown sugar to the heated glass, fill with hot coffee, and stir for 15 seconds until the sugar dissolves.

3. Whisk together the heavy cream and vanilla paste until soft peaks form. Top the drink with at least 1 inch of the vanilla cloud cream.

Haunted Halloween Punch (Mocktail)

1 Granny Smith apple, unpeeled and sliced

2 oranges, unpeeled and sliced

2 limes, unpeeled and sliced

6 sprigs of fresh mint, divided

1 cup Trader Joe's 100% Cherry Juice

1 cup Trader Joe's Apple Juice

1 cup Trader Joe's 100% Cranberry Juice

1 cup grapefruit juice

2 cups prepared Trader Joe's Organic Blood Orange Rooibos Herbal Tea Blend using 2 bags

1 cup Trader Joe's Sparkling Apple Cider

Trader Joe's Fruit Jellies, for garnish

⇒⋅⇐

YIELD: 6 drinks

Inspired by the playful traditions of Halloween and the vibrant colors of autumn, this nonalcoholic punch is a festive blend of fruity flavors and ghoulish garnishes. The addition of tea and grapefruit transforms what might be a standard Halloween punch into a sophisticated mocktail. Garnish with fruit jellies or other gummy candies.

1. Add the slices of apple, oranges, and limes along with 3 sprigs of the mint to a pitcher or punch bowl. Pour in all the juices and stir. Refrigerate for 1 to 4 hours.

2. Brew the tea and allow to cool.

3. Strain out the fruit and mint, and discard.

4. Add the cooled tea and cider to the strained punch and stir.

5. Add ice to a punch glass, fill with punch, and garnish with the remaining mint and the gummy candies on the rim.

Dirty Ginger (Mocktail)

2 pieces Trader Joe's Crystallized Candied Ginger, divided

2 ounces Trader Joe's Spiced Chai Black Tea Concentrate

½ ounce brewed and chilled Trader Joe's Shade Grown Espresso Blend

1 ounce heavy cream

YIELD: 1 drink

Warm your senses with this mocktail, an invigorating blend of chai spices, heavy cream, and bold espresso. Inspired by the traditional Indian flavored tea beverage known as masala chai, this drink is a cool refresher while adding spice to your autumnal gatherings.

1. Cut 1 piece of the candied ginger roughly and add it to a shaker. Add the chai concentrate, and crush with a muddler or wooden spoon for 30 seconds.

2. Fill three-quarters full with ice and add the espresso and heavy cream. Shake for 15 to 25 seconds.

3. Strain into a coupe glass and lay thin strips of the remaining piece of candied ginger over the rim of the glass.

WINTER

Warming Wassail Punch with Cloven Oranges

6 cinnamon sticks

6 green cardamom pods or 1 teaspoon ground cardamom

6 whole cloves plus more for studding oranges

½ teaspoon ground nutmeg

6 cups Trader Joe's Winter Wassail Punch

1 (750-ml) bottle Trader Joe's Grand Reserve Willamette Valley Pinot Noir Lot 124

2 (750-ml) bottles Trader Joe's Reserve Santa Ynez Valley GSM Lot 248

2 oranges

1½ cups Trader Joe's Kentucky Bourbon Straight Whiskey

2 bags Trader Joe's English Breakfast Tea

3 tablespoons Spiced Syrup (page 72)

6 dashes Trader Joe's Classic Bitters

YIELD: about 20 drinks

From the Old English for "be in good health," wassail is the perfect way to toast your friends during the winter holidays. Wassail is a classic mulled wine or cider that has been spiked with warming spices. This punch is perfect for a party and uses one of Trader Joe's favorite holiday drinks and some extra spices, wine, and whiskey to keep you singing and toasting through the night.

1. In a large dry stockpot or enameled cast-iron Dutch oven over medium-high heat, toast the cinnamon, cardamom, cloves, and nutmeg until fragrant, 30 to 60 seconds. Add the Winter Wassail Punch and the two wines. Bring to a simmer, then reduce the heat to low.

2. Cut the oranges into ½-inch slices and stud with additional cloves. Drop the cloven oranges into the punch. Cook for at least 30 minutes to marry the flavors.

3. Add the bourbon, tea bags, spiced syrup, and bitters 5 minutes before you serve.

4. Keep the punch warm on the stovetop at your lowest setting. Remove the tea bags and ladle into a punch glass with pieces of the cloven oranges and cinnamon sticks.

The Dirtiest Martini

2½ ounces Trader Joe's Art of the Still Organic Gin

½ ounce dry vermouth

¼ ounce olive brine

¼ ounce caper vinegar

Trader Joe's Capers in Vinegar, for garnish

Trader Joe's Cambozola Triple Cream Soft Ripened Blue Cheese, for garnish

Trader Joe's Blue Cheese Stuffed Chalkidiki Olives, for garnish

YIELD: 1 drink

If you like your drinks with a savory kick, then a dirty martini is your new best friend. What makes a martini dirty is the addition of olive brine and some amazing garnishes. Olives overstuffed with blue cheese and briny capers pair perfectly with the botanical notes of gin to make this dirtiest of all martinis. Some people use vodka to make a dirty martini, but gin plays better with the salty accompaniments.

1. Create the garnish by draining the olives and capers, reserving their brine. Cut three ½-inch pieces of cheese and add to the filling of 3 olives. Press a caper into the cheese of each olive and skewer the olives. Place in a chilled coupe or martini glass.

2. Fill a shaker three-quarters full with ice, and add the gin, vermouth, olive brine, and caper vinegar. Shake for 15 to 25 seconds and strain into the glass.

Sage and Blackberry Sour

SAGE SYRUP

3 sprigs of fresh sage

½ cup sugar

½ cup water

COCKTAIL

1½ ounces Trader Joe's Art of the Still Organic Gin

¾ ounce lemon juice

6 blackberries

1 egg white

2 dashes Trader Joe's Classic Bitters

YIELD: 1 drink

Winter may be chilly, but Trader Joe's has great produce year-round to enjoy. This take on the classic sour blends tart blackberries with the earthy vegetal notes of sage to create a striking and fragrant cocktail. If you want a vegan version, substitute aquafaba (the liquid from canned chickpeas that whips up just as light) for the egg white.

1. To make the sage syrup: Add the sage, sugar, and water to a small saucepan. Bring to a boil, then reduce to medium-low and simmer for 5 minutes. Remove from the heat and allow to come to room temperature. Strain out the sage and refrigerate.

2. To make the cocktail: Add the gin, lemon juice, blackberries, egg white, and bitters along with 1 ounce of the sage syrup to a shaker without ice and shake for 20 seconds.

3. Fill the shaker three-quarters full with ice, and shake for an additional 15 to 25 seconds and strain into a chilled rocks glass.

Burnt Orange Negroni

¾ ounce Trader Joe's Art of the Still Organic Gin

¾ ounce Campari

¾ ounce sweet vermouth

peel from 1 orange

YIELD: 1 drink

Named for Count Camillo Negroni, who first requested the addition of gin to his Americano cocktail in the early 20th century, the Negroni has become a beloved classic thanks to its timeless elegance and complex flavor profile. There are many ways to add smoky notes to a drink, but the simplest is to ignite the oils in a citrus peel held over the drink.

1. Fill a rocks glass halfway with ice.

2. Add the gin, Campari, and vermouth. Stir for 20 to 30 seconds.

3. Cut a large round piece of orange peel, about 2 inches wide, with as little white pith as possible. Hold it over the glass. Light a match and quickly squeeze the zest, squirting orange oil that will flame. This will give a slightly caramelized orange taste to the cocktail. Drop the peel in the glass and serve.

Violet Royale

1 ounce crème de violette

½ ounce Trader Joe's Limoncello Sicilian Liquor

1 dash Trader Joe's Classic Bitters

½ ounce lemon juice

2 to 3 ounces chilled La Burgondie Crémant de Bourgogne Brut Reserve

YIELD: 1 drink

Based on the classic French aperitif Kir Royal, this champagne cocktail uses crème de violette instead of crème de cassis for a lighter flavor, and limoncello for balanced sweetness. This drink is a stunner during winter holiday brunches.

1. Pour the crème de violette, limoncello, bitters, and lemon juice in a mixing glass filled with ice, and stir for 20 to 30 seconds.

2. Strain into a chilled champagne flute, and fill with the sparkling wine.

Mexican Chocolate Martini

½ ounce Trader Joe's Organic Midnight Moo Chocolate Syrup plus more for garnish

1 ounce crème de cacao

2 ounces Trader Joe's TX Vodka

1 ounce brewed and chilled Trader Joe's Shade Grown Ground Espresso Blend

½ ounce heavy cream

pinch of salt

¼ teaspoon Trader Joe's Bourbon Vanilla Bean Paste

Trader Joe's Pound Plus 72% Cacao Dark Chocolate Bar, for garnish

YIELD: 1 drink

The chocolate martini has been done to death, but this take on it cuts down on the sugar and elevates the spice. Inspired by the traditional Mexican hot chocolate known as champurrado, *this cocktail is a celebration of the rich flavors and vibrant culture of Mexico.*

1. Using a paintbrush, paint a streak of chocolate syrup from top to bottom inside a chilled martini glass.

2. To a shaker filled three-quarters with ice, add the chocolate syrup, crème de cacao, vodka, espresso, heavy cream, salt, and vanilla. Shake for 15 to 20 seconds.

3. Strain into the martini glass.

4. To garnish, using your hand, warm one side of the bar of chocolate slightly (this will make for much better curls). With a vegetable peeler, make curls by slowly and firmly scraping down the warmed edge of the chocolate. Place on top of the martini.

Cold Brew White Russian

2 ounces Trader Joe's Small Batch Vodka Distilled 10 Times

1 ounce Trader Joe's Ready to Drink Cold Brew Coffee

1 ounce coffee liqueur

1 ounce heavy cream

YIELD: 1 drink

As anyone who loved movies in the 1990s knows, the Dude always abides with the help of a stiff cocktail. This White Russian adds another layer of bitter notes by incorporating cold brew coffee, which has a higher caffeine content and less harsh tannins, perfect to complement this rich drink.

1. Add the vodka, coffee, and coffee liqueur to a rocks glass with a large ice cube.

2. Stir for 20 to 30 seconds, and top with the heavy cream.

Tootsy Roll Shot

1 ounce Trader Joes Cold Pressed Orange Juice

1½ ounces coffee liqueur

YIELD: 1 drink

Shot enthusiasts love a good shot that has ingredients that shouldn't go together but, when paired, create something totally unique. Blending orange juice with coffee liqueur produces a chocolatey, sugary drink that evokes memories of childhood sweets with a much more grown-up effect.

1. To a shaker filled three-quarters with ice, add the orange juice and coffee liqueur.

2. Shake for 15 to 25 seconds, then strain into a shot glass.

Dark and Stormy Night

4 ounces Trader Joe's Triple Ginger Brew

2 ounces Trader Joe's White Rum of the Gods

1 lime, for juice and garnish

YIELD: 1 drink

This traditional Bermudian cocktail dating back to the early 20th century is all about the ginger beer. Now is not the time for a can of ginger ale. This three-ingredient drink relies on the intensely flavored Trader Joe's Triple Ginger Brew and just the right amount of effervescence to play off the caramel tones of the rum.

1. Fill a Collins glass with ice and pour in the ginger brew.

2. Top with the rum and a squeeze of lime.

3. Lightly stir the drink and garnish with a lime wheel on the rim of the glass.

Punchy Pomegranate Punch

1 (12-ounce) can Trader Joe's Sparkling Pomegranate Punch Beverage

1½ ounces Trader Joe's Small Batch Vodka Distilled 10 Times

½ ounce pomegranate liqueur

½ ounce fresh lime juice

1 tablespoon Trader Joe's Sweetened Dried Cranberries

1 lemon, for garnish

YIELD: 1 drink

When throwing a party, combining premade and fresh ingredients to create easy libations for your guests can be a massive time and stress saver. This punch relies on one of Trader Joe's classic seasonal canned drinks. Feel free to try different sparkling beverages to customize this punch to your palate and the season.

1. To a wine glass, add the sparkling pomegranate punch, vodka, pomegranate liqueur, lime juice, and sweetened dried cranberries.

2. Stir and garnish with a piece of lemon zest.

French 76

MEYER LEMON SYRUP

1 Meyer lemon

½ cup sugar

½ cup water

COCKTAIL

2 ounces Trader Joe's Art of the Still Organic Gin

½ ounce fresh Meyer lemon juice

4 ounces chilled Charles de Marques Brut Champagne

Meyer lemon twist, for garnish

YIELD: 1 drink plus additional syrup

Raise a glass to elegance and sophistication with a French 76, a timeless blend of gin, lemon juice, sugar, and champagne. A step-up from the French 75 cocktail, named for a powerful artillery piece used by France in World War I, this version relies on Meyer lemon to create a sweeter, lighter sparkler.

1. To make the Meyer lemon syrup: Cut a twist from the zest of the lemon, then juice it. Save ½ ounce of the juice and the twist for the cocktail. Roughly chop the juiced lemon and add it, along with the remaining juice, sugar, and water, to a small saucepan.

2. To make the cocktail: Fill a shaker three-quarters full of ice, and add the gin, the reserved Meyer lemon juice, and ½ ounce of the Meyer lemon syrup. Shake for 15 to 25 seconds. Strain into a chilled flute and top with the champagne. Garnish with the Meyer lemon twist.

Smoky Ghosty (Mocktail)

¼ cup frozen Trader Joe's Mango Chunks

¼ cup Trader Joe's 100% Mango Juice

⅛ teaspoon kosher salt

¼ teaspoon ground cardamom

¼ cup heavy cream

2 tablespoons dark brown sugar

⅛ teaspoon Trader Joe's Smoked Ghost Chilies

¼ cup brewed and chilled Joe Medium Roast Ground Coffee

YIELD: 1 drink

Mocktails often can be simple and sweet. Not this drink! The combination of sweet mango, bitter coffee, and spicy smoked ghost pepper really makes for a complex cocktail that will unfold itself to you as you enjoy it. The fiery pepper may sound intense, but when used sparingly and tamed with the mango and heavy cream, the drink is perfectly balanced.

1. In a blender, combine the frozen mango chunks, juice, salt, and cardamom. Blend until smooth.

2. Whisk together the heavy cream, brown sugar, and smoked ghost pepper powder until soft peaks form.

3. Assemble the drink in a rocks glass. Pour the mango mixture into the bottom of the glass, add the chilled coffee, and top with the peppery whipped cream.

Gooseberry Starfruit Refresher (Mocktail)

6 Trader Joe's Cape Gooseberries

1 (12-ounce) can Trader Joe's Starfruit Sparkling Water

YIELD: 1 drink

Two underutilized fruits are the star players in the winter months at Trader Joe's. This two-ingredient spritz marries gooseberries, which look like golden orbs of sunshine and taste like tangy grapes, and starfruit, a beautiful fruit with a delicate sweet-and-sour flavor.

1. In the bottom of a Collins glass, add 6 gooseberries and crush them with a muddler or wooden spoon to release their juices.

2. Fill the glass with ice, and top with the sparkling water.

DRINKS INDEX

ACKNOWLEDGMENTS

This book could not have happened without my art director, Eponine McBoat, who made everything look amazing, and my partner, Rebecca Howard, who organized, prepped, and shopped for me.

A huge thank you to my editor Kierra Sondereker, who has made this book better than I could have ever imagined, and my copyeditor, Susan Lang, who is the reason why this book is readable. I'd also to acknowledge the hard work of the entire Ulysses team, including Claire Chun, Renee Rutledge, and Barbara Schultz.

I came to this book only through my decades-long collaboration with my writing partner, Allyson Reedy, who has journeyed with me through writing, designing, and publishing.

And of course, to my love, Trader Joe's, which provided me with amazing products for my crazy, harebrained ideas.

ABOUT THE AUTHOR

Greg McBoat first watched Julia Child making her Queen of Sheba cake when he was six years old. He was captivated by her style of explaining the history and influence of food and drink. This began Greg's understanding of how the stories behind food and drinks give unique insights into people and cultures. His mission is to change people's lives through the stories he tells.

While specializing in food and drink photography and writing, Greg has worked for such clients as *Food and Wine*, the *Denver Post*, Joseph Phelps Winery, and Hard Rock Cafe. Greg has collaborated on three previous cookbooks: *50 Things to Bake Before You Die*, *The Official Catan Cookbook*, and *The Official Ticket* to *Ride Cookbook*. Greg is from New Mexico and lives in Denver, Colorado, with his daughter, Eponine, and cat, Ash.